Disney
MALEFICENT

Level 6

Re-told by: Lynda Edwards
Series Editor: Rachel Wilson

T0345779

Contents

In This Book

Maleficent

The strongest fairy, who becomes the Protector of the Moors

Stefan

Maleficent's friend, who wanted to be king

Princess Aurora

A happy and kind child. Maleficent calls her "Beastie"

Diaval

A black bird who changes into a man, and different animals, with Maleficent's magic

The Flower Pixies

The king asks them to look after Aurora when she is a child

The Moors

A beautiful land where fairies and magical creatures live

Before You Read

Introduction

The land of humans and the land of the Fair Folk, which is called the Moors, have always been enemies. Greedy kings have wanted to own this beautiful land. Now it is dangerous for the Fair Folk to go into the human land, or for humans to go into the Moors. There is a story that one day a strong leader will bring the two lands together in peace. One day, a young fairy and a human boy become friends, but who is the hero and who is the villain? Will peace ever come to these lands?

Activities

1 **Read *In This Book* and answer the questions.**

1 Who do you think is the hero?

2 Who do you think is the villain?

3 Who do you think will fall in love?

4 Who do you think will change their ideas during the story?

2 **Choose the correct words. You can use the *Glossary*.**

1 *Fairies / Humans* have wings and can do magic.

2 People catch fish in a *chain / net*.

3 If a fairy *curses / kisses* you, something bad will happen.

4 *Iron / Peace* is a metal.

5 Some flowers have sharp *thorns / needles*.

1 A Strange Meeting

This is a story about two lands. They were neighbors but they were also great enemies.

In one country, the people were humans. Some people were poor and were farmers. Others were rich and lived in castles. Their king, Henry, was a greedy man.

The other country was the Moors and it was a land of fairy folk. There, the trees, valleys, and pools were alive with all kinds of strange and wonderful creatures.

A young fairy called Maleficent lived in this magical place. Her happy smile brought light and love to the land and all the creatures.

King Henry wanted the Moors. He, like his father and his grandfather, wanted to own the beautiful land and everything in it. He was ready to fight to get it, but the fairies were strong, and they had magic.

These lands needed to become friends. They needed a strong leader to bring peace.

This is the story of that leader, too.

Maleficent was excited. A human boy in the Moors! Humans never came here. The guards saw him taking stones from the pool. The boy looked scared.

"It's not right to steal," Maleficent said softly, and she led him out of the Moors. They were both quiet. It was strange for a human and a fairy to meet.

The boy's name was Stefan. He pointed to a castle. "One day I'll live there." Then he smiled. "We'll see each other again."

"Perhaps," Maleficent said shyly. Stefan touched her fingers, but his iron ring burned her. Iron was dangerous for Maleficent.

"I'm sorry!" Stefan threw away the ring and started to walk away. Then he turned. "I like your wings!" he shouted.

Maleficent laughed. Her fairy friends were wrong. Not *all* humans were dangerous.

◇———◇

Maleficent, the fairy, and Stefan, the human, became good friends. They met in the Moors and played and laughed together. Time passed and they grew older.

On Maleficent's sixteenth birthday, Stefan gave her a kiss. He called it "True Love's Kiss" because it was real and honest. Stefan first stole a stone, and then he stole a fairy's heart.

2 A Fight for Power

Stefan's dream to live in the castle was very strong. Maleficent waited for his visits, but he didn't come. She often sat alone in the dark. She was now the Protector of the Moors, but she still didn't understand why humans were so greedy.

In his big castle, King Henry heard about the strong fairy in the Moors. He became afraid of her power and he decided to attack.

Maleficent heard the sound of horses on the ground. They were getting closer to the Moors. She knew it meant danger and she flew to meet it.

"We're not afraid of magical creatures!" King Henry shouted to his men. "We will take the Moors!"

Suddenly, there was a strange wind and the men looked up. It was Maleficent's dark wings. She flew down and stood in front of Henry.

"Stop!" she cried.

"A king does not take orders from a fairy," Henry laughed.

"You are no king to me!" Maleficent said.

"Bring me her head," Henry shouted, and his men rode toward Maleficent. But the fairy didn't move. She lifted her arms.

"Rise and stand with me!" she called.

The horses were afraid when the ground opened in front of them. Strange creatures rose from the holes. There were trees with arms, and wild animals with sharp teeth. A snake with a body of leaves and earth rose in the air. The horses screamed as the creatures moved toward them.

The fight was short. Horses fell. Men hit the ground and died. Maleficent flew at King Henry and her wings knocked him from his horse.

The fairy put her face close to his. "You will never have the Moors!" she cried.

Maleficent thanked her friends. The Moors were safe—for now.

King Henry was dying. He lay in bed with his most important men around him.

"I see you're waiting for me to die," he said angrily. "But what then?" King Henry only had a daughter. He grew weaker and Stefan helped to lift his head.

"I promised the people that one day we would take the Moors," King Henry whispered. Then he gave the men another promise. The person who destroyed the winged creature would be king after him.

Stefan knew it was his time to act.

"How is life with the humans?" Maleficent asked Stefan coldly.

"They are horrible. They mean to hurt you!" Stefan told her.

Maleficent and Stefan talked for a long time. Then she drank from Stefan's bottle and immediately fell deeply asleep.

Stefan did not sleep. He lifted a knife above the fairy, but then threw it down angrily. He couldn't destroy her. But what should he do? He wanted to be king! He looked at Maleficent's beautiful wings, and he had his answer. He took out an iron chain …

Stefan put Maleficent's heavy wings on Henry's bed. King Henry was pleased. Now, he could die in peace. "You have done well."

Yes, thought Stefan. Now I've got my dream.

3 Maleficent's Curse

Maleficent woke up and felt a terrible pain. Her wings were gone. Her cry became a scream when she realized that she could never fly again. Stefan did this, she thought. *Why?* He was her friend.

Slowly she stood up, but it was difficult to walk. She found a stick and finally, she reached an old castle. It was only broken walls of stone, but she decided to stay there. It was dark, like her heart. From there she could see Stefan's castle. It rose tall and proud against the night sky. Maleficent's body and heart grew colder.

The next day, a farmer caught a black bird in a net. It fought hard to escape and Maleficent watched. Then she had an idea. "Into a man," she said softly. Her magic changed the bird into a person, and he quickly pulled off the net.

"What have you done?" he said. The bird-man's name was Diaval, and at first it felt strange for him to be a man. But then he thanked Maleficent for saving his life and told her that he would do anything for her.

The fairy's eyes shone. "Wings. I need you to be my wings."

From a window high in the castle wall, Diaval saw Stefan in the King's clothes. He told Maleficent.

"He did this to me so that he would be King," she screamed. Green fire rose from her hands and into the sky. Stefan saw it from his castle.

Then Maleficent walked across the Moors and the land became dark behind her. The creatures hid from her angry face. Her magic made a chair of thorns and she sat like Stefan, queen of a dark country.

⊸——⊸

One day, Diaval told Maleficent about a new baby.

It was the name day for the new princess and music welcomed people from many lands. The great room was full. The baby, Aurora, lay in her bed and smiled at everyone.

Suddenly, the room grew quiet and three strange creatures flew through the crowd toward the king. They were pixies who wanted peace between the two lands. They brought magical presents for the princess. The first pixie wished for the baby to grow up beautiful. The second wished for her always to be happy. The third started, "I wish that she …," but then a fierce wind moved through the room.

Maleficent was standing at the entrance. She walked toward Stefan with a cold smile. The crowd grew silent.

Stefan was scared. "You are not welcome here."

"Not welcome?" Maleficent smiled. "But I also have a gift for the princess."

Green smoke started to rise from her hands. "Listen well. Aurora will be beautiful, and everyone will love her, but …," she looked at Stefan with hard, empty eyes. "On her sixteenth birthday she will hurt her finger on a spindle, and she will go into a deep sleep. She will never wake!"

"Maleficent!" Stefan cried. "Please, please don't do this!"

Maleficent smiled. "I like that," she said. "Ask me again."

Stefan was a proud man, but he went down on his knees. "Please Maleficent, please no."

Maleficent stood above him and lifted her arms. "I accept. The princess can wake, but only ...," the fairy looked straight at Stefan and her eyes were burning, "by True Love's Kiss. This curse will last until the end of time. No power on Earth can ever change it!"

Then, in a cloud of green smoke, she disappeared.

Immediately, Stefan ordered his men to break every spindle in the castle. They put the pieces in a locked room that was deep under the ground. Stefan gave Aurora to the three pixies. He told them to take Aurora to a secret house. They must look after her until her sixteenth birthday. He was going to protect his child from Maleficent's terrible curse.

Stefan knew now, he had to destroy Maleficent. But the strong fairy built a dark wall of trees around the Moors. Sharp, black thorns grew from them.

No human will ever come into the Moors again, she promised.

 4 Stefan Plans

In their forest house, the pixies tried to be like humans. They changed their shape and stopped using magic. It wasn't easy and they fought a lot!

Secretly, Maleficent visited the house at night and looked through the window at the baby.

"Oh—it's so ugly I could almost feel sorry for it," she said. Aurora saw Maleficent and smiled. "I hate you!" Maleficent said fiercely, but Aurora smiled again.

The pixies tried hard to be good aunts to Aurora, but they didn't know much about babies and sometimes they forgot about her completely!

Aurora cried a lot because she was hungry. Maleficent hated the noise and finally ordered Diaval to fly to the baby with food. He took a flower and Aurora happily drank the sugar water. The crying stopped.

And so Diaval and Maleficent helped baby Aurora to grow up. The child was always happy and smiling and Maleficent's hard heart became softer. She used her magic to do fun things, not horrible ones. She sometimes played games on the pixies. One day, it started raining inside the house on the pixies' heads!

Maleficent watched and laughed. This was *fun*.

In his castle, Stefan could only think about one thing—destroying Maleficent.

His men shot balls of fire into the wall of thorns but Maleficent sent the fire back. The burning trees grew tall and fell down on them.

"We cannot burn the wall!" one of Stefan's men told him.

Stefan was angry. Nothing was impossible. He hit the table with his knife. Then he looked at the knife, and slowly an idea came into his head. He remembered when his ring burned Maleficent's hand. He turned to the man.

"Bring me the iron-workers," he said quietly.

One day, Aurora was following a butterfly and nearly fell down into a river. Maleficent used her magic to catch the child.

Aurora saw the fairy and laughed. She put her arms around Maleficent's legs.

"Go away!" Maleficent said angrily. "I don't like children!" But Aurora didn't go, and finally Maleficent lifted her up. Her small body was warm.

Stefan often sat alone and looked at Maleficent's wings. They were in a glass case. Light from the small window shone through and they seemed alive.

"When the curse fails, Maleficent will come for me," he whispered. "And on that day, I will be ready."

5 Aurora Learns About her Past

Aurora grew into a beautiful, happy, and kind young girl, who loved the forest and all its animals. She often stood in front of the wall of thorns and tried to see through to the world behind.

⬦———⬦

One evening, Maleficent put Aurora into a deep sleep and her magic lifted the girl into the air. The thorn trees let Maleficent and the sleeping Aurora through. The princess woke up beside a pool that shone with dancing lights. She couldn't breathe. Magic was everywhere. Fairies with shining tails flew out of the water. This world was like a dream.

Then she saw Maleficent. "I know you!" she cried, excitedly. "You're my Fairy Godmother! I've always known you were close by."

Maleficent lifted her hand and Aurora was asleep again. When Aurora was safely back in her bed, Maleficent smiled. "Goodnight, Beastie," she whispered.

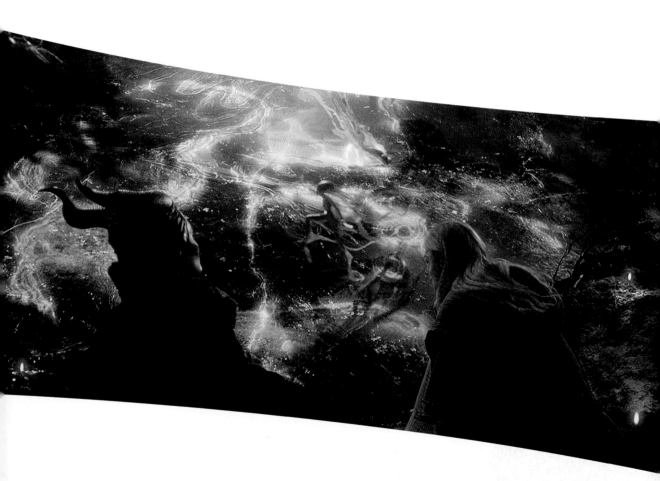

After that, Maleficent often brought Aurora to the Moors at night. They sat together and watched as the fairies danced through the trees. The princess's smile brought light into the dark land and touched Maleficent's cold heart.

It was nearly Aurora's sixteenth birthday and Maleficent stood beside the princess's bed. She knew she needed to act.

She lifted her hands and the green smoke rose from them. "I take back my curse!" she cried, and the air filled with magic. "I take back my curse!" she screamed.

The green smoke burned around the bed, but then Maleficent heard her own words from sixteen years ago. *No power on Earth can stop this.* She knew she could change nothing. Her curse was too strong.

Maleficent tried to tell Aurora about the curse. "I had wings once,"' she said sadly. "But a human stole them from me. There is evil in the world. I cannot keep you safe from it ..."

"I have a plan," Aurora smiled. "One day I shall come to live in the Moors with you forever. You can look after me!"

Maleficent looked at the girl's happy face and her heart lifted. "Come now!"

Aurora was excited and ran to tell her aunts. She stopped in the forest to practice her words. It was going to be difficult. Her aunts loved her.

Aurora heard a noise and turned. A handsome young man was getting off his horse. He told Aurora that his name was Phillip.

"I'm on my way to King Stefan's castle. Can you help me?" Surprised, Aurora moved back quickly and fell.

"Forgive me!" Phillip helped her stand. Then time seemed to stop. They couldn't move. Something strange was happening.

Finally, Aurora pointed toward the castle. Her face felt warm. "Will you be back?" she asked.

Phillip smiled, "Nothing could stop me."

"That boy is the answer," Diaval said. "True Love's Kiss, remember?" Maleficent didn't smile. There was no True Love's Kiss.

"I'll be sixteen tomorrow," Aurora said with a big smile. "I'm leaving home!"

"Oh no you aren't!" the aunts shouted angrily. "We are taking you back to your father ..."

"You told me my parents were dead!" cried the princess.

Then the pixies told her about the evil fairy and her curse. When Aurora realized that it was Maleficent, she started to cry. She turned and ran. She ran away from the forest and away from the Moors. She ran to the castle and to her father, Stefan.

"Find the boy!" Maleficent told Diaval.

6 True Love's Kiss

"A day too soon!" Stefan shouted. "Lock her up in her room!" In his head, the voice whispered *She's coming.*

Aurora couldn't think clearly and there was a strange pain in her finger. She walked around and around the room until she found a secret door. She went through it. Something was pulling her forward. Her finger was redder and hurting badly.

Suddenly, there was a heavy door in front of her. It opened and Aurora walked into a dark room full of broken spindles. Green fire moved over the pieces and made a new spindle. Its needle was long and shining …

Maleficent found Phillip and put him into a magical sleep. Diaval, now a horse, carried him and they rode fast toward the castle.

A voice whispered *Aurora. Aurora.* The princess walked slowly toward the bright needle. She reached out her hand and touched it. Then, the world went black and Aurora fell to the floor.

A fierce wind pushed dark clouds across the sky and Maleficent's horse screamed.

Stefan looked down at his daughter. "She's only sleeping!" the pixies said. "What about the kiss? True Love's Kiss!"
    "True Love?" Stefan laughed. There was no True Love!

There was a wall of sharp, iron thorns around the castle, but they didn't stop Maleficent. She moved carefully between them, with Diaval and Phillip.

Inside the castle, they found Aurora's room.

Phillip looked at the sleeping princess. "She is the most beautiful girl I've ever seen!" he said softly.

"Kiss her," said the pixies.

"I don't—," said Phillip.

"Kiss her!"

The boy kissed Aurora, and no one breathed. Could his kiss wake her up?

The princess's eyes stayed closed. No. It wasn't True Love's Kiss.

Maleficent walked quietly to the bed and sadly looked down at the lovely face.

"I did something terrible," she thought, "because I was young, and I was lost. Then you, Aurora, you stole my heart, and now I have lost you forever." Maleficent was crying. She kissed Aurora's hair. She turned from the bed slowly but then she stopped.

"Hello, Godmother," Aurora's eyes were open.

"True love," said Diaval quietly.

"Hello, Beastie," Maleficent smiled.

Maleficent led Aurora through the castle, but in one room they heard a strange noise. Maleficent looked up. Something heavy and dark was falling from the ceiling.

"Ahh!" Maleficent screamed as an iron net closed over her.

7 Escape from the Castle

Maleficent tried to fight the net but her whole body was burning with pain. "Run, Aurora," she cried. The girl must not see her die like this.

Stefan's men attacked Maleficent from all sides with their iron sticks. She couldn't escape them, and she grew weaker. Then, she saw Diaval and reached her fingers through the net. "Into a dragon," she whispered.

A great noise filled the room and the men turned. They looked up into the teeth of a dragon and felt the heat from its breath. The fire burned them, and its wings threw them against the walls.

Then, its teeth pulled back the net from Maleficent. She stood but she was very weak.

Immediately, more men ran in and threw chains over the dragon. The creature couldn't move. The men circled Maleficent and hit the floor with their iron sticks.

Stefan came into the circle. Iron clothes covered his body and he carried iron chains. Maleficent could only see his eyes and they were cold and empty.

"How does it feel? To be a fairy creature without wings?" he laughed and then threw his chain around her. She fell and he pulled her across the floor. Maleficent knew she was losing the fight.

Aurora ran. The fire, the screams, and the fighting filled her head. She ran into a small room and saw a glass case with something dark inside. Were they Maleficent's wings? Aurora pushed the case to the floor and it broke. Immediately, there was a loud *Whoosh*.

Stefan pulled out an iron knife and moved toward Maleficent. The fairy was on her knees. Her eyes were cloudy. Stefan was just a dark shape in front of her. Suddenly, a bright light shone across his face and Maleficent felt something heavy on her shoulders. It was a weight that she remembered well.

Maleficent rose into the air. "No," she thought. "This fight is not over." She attacked.

Together, the dragon and the fairy fought Stefan's men, and soon bodies covered the floor. Then, Stefan's chain caught Maleficent's foot and she couldn't get free.

His cold eyes smiled, and he started to pull the fairy down, but Maleficent smiled, too. Her strong wings lifted Stefan into the air, and they went through the big window. He screamed as he held onto the end of the chain.

Maleficent flew down to a stone bridge. She put her hands around her enemy's neck …

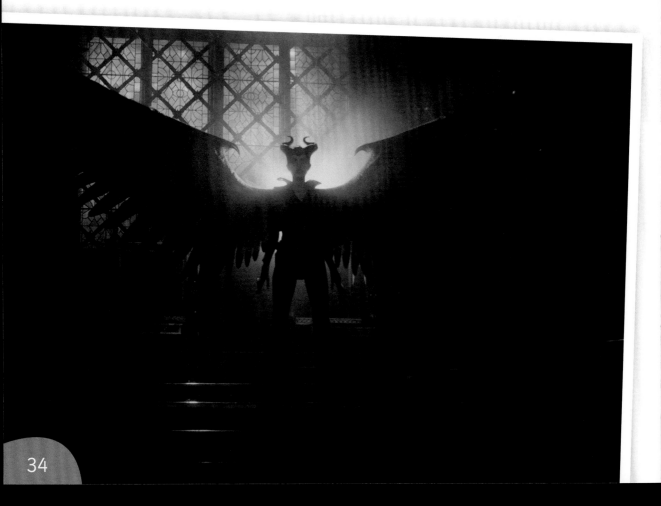

"You won't hurt me," Stefan said. "I'm Aurora's father!"

Maleficent looked at him and she knew he was right. Her love for Aurora was stronger than her hatred for this man. She turned away. Stefan fought to breathe again. Then, with a loud cry, he ran at Maleficent from behind. Together, they fell from the bridge. Stefan's arms held Maleficent's wings closed. They fell, faster and faster toward the Earth until finally the fairy's wings opened. They lifted her before they hit the ground.

Stefan's luck was over. He was still reaching up for Maleficent when he died.

8 A New Ending

The sun rose over the castle and Aurora and Phillip watched it from the Moors. There was no wall of thorns, and the land was alive and bright with magic again.

Sunlight brought flowers to the dead, dark trees, and fairy wings shone silver in the air.

The pixies put flowers in Aurora's hair. "You have your queen," Maleficent said to the crowd of magical creatures.

So, now we know the real end of the old story. The person who brought peace to the two lands was neither a hero nor a villain. She was both—and her name was Maleficent.

After You Read

1 **Put the story into the correct order.**

a Maleficent builds a wall of thorns.

b Aurora touches the spindle.

c Maleficent helps Diaval escape the farmer's net.

d Diaval becomes a dragon.

e Maleficent fights Henry to protect the Moors.

f Maleficent curses Aurora.

g Stefan cuts off Maleficent's wings.

2 **Who says these things? Why do they say it?**

Aurora   Diaval   Henry   Maleficent   Phillip   Stefan

1 "One day I'll live there."

2 "You are no king to me!

3 "You have done well."

4 "That boy is the answer."

5 "You can look after me."

6 "Nothing could stop me!"

3 **Answer the questions.**

1 Who is your favorite character in the story? Why?

2 Did you like the end of the story? Why / why not?

3 How did Maleficent and Stefan change during the story?

4 What do you think is the main message of the story?

Glossary

chain (*noun*) a lot of metal rings that join together

creature (*noun*) an animal that is either real or imagined

curse (*noun*) words that bring bad luck

dragon (*noun*) a big, imaginary animal that has wings, a long tail, and can breathe fire

evil (*adj.*) very bad; very wrong

fairy (*noun*) a magical creature like a small person, with wings

human (*noun*) a man, woman, or child

iron (*noun*) a hard metal

kiss (*noun*) a touch from someone's mouth; *On Maleficent's sixteenth birthday, Stefan gave her a kiss.*

lift past tense **lifted** (*verb*) to move something up into the air with your hands; *Maleficent lifted her hand and Aurora was asleep again.*

like (*prep.*) nearly the same as something

magic (*noun*) a power that makes strange or impossible things happen

needle (*noun*) a small, thin piece of metal that is sharp

net (*noun*) something that people use for catching animals

peace (*noun*) a time when there isn't any fighting

protect past tense **protected** (*verb*) to look after people or places and stop people hurting them; *He was going to protect his child from Maleficent's terrible curse.*

safe (*adj.*) not in danger

spindle (*noun*) a round stick which is sharp at one end for making wool into thread

thorn (*noun*) sharp things that grow on some plants and can hurt you

whisper past tense **whispered** (*verb*) to speak very quietly; *A voice whispered Aurora.*

Play: Protectors of Nature

Scene 1:

A farmer and his young son are sitting on a stone wall in the fields. They're watching their sheep and eating some supper. The father takes his piece of cake and puts it on the ground.

SON: [surprised] You don't want your sweet cake, Papa?

FATHER: I'm leaving it here for the Fair Folk. To thank them for making the grass grow tall. And to show them we're *friendly* humans.

SON: [very surprised] Fairies aren't *real*, Papa!

FATHER: Yes, they are, Son. They're a part of nature. They look after the plants, the animals, even the air itself. But some humans don't care about that.

SON: What do you mean?

FATHER: Well, some people attack their lands. They want to take these gifts of nature for themselves. Oh, there's been plenty of trouble between greedy humans and the Fair Folk over the years.

SON: Have you ever seen a fairy, Papa? What do they look like?

FATHER: [jumping off the wall] Come on, now. Enough questions for one day.

Scene 2:

The farmer and his son are walking home.

SON: [pointing] Is that a fairy, Papa?

FATHER: [smiling] No, that's a butterfly. The Fair Folk live over there, in the Moors.

SON: [stopping to look] Oh, there are so many big trees …

FATHER: [walking on] Come on! Mother's waiting for us.

Global Citizenship

Protect the Forests

Rosamira Guillen is a conservationist from Colombia. She started a group called Fundación Proyecto Tití to protect the Cotton-top Tamarin and its environment. The Cotton-top Tamarin is a kind of monkey that lives only in Colombia. It is endangered because some people are burning or cutting down trees to make money. This is called deforestation and the tamarin's home is disappearing. Other people want to take and sell the tamarin as illegal pets.

Rosamira protects the tamarin and the forest by teaching people about them. She wants people to know what is happening to them. If more people know, then they can work together to save the tamarin and its environment.

Rosamira also helps people who live near the tamarin. If they can make money in different ways, then the tamarin can live in peace. The people sell bags made from recycled plastic they find in the forest.

Find Out

What do you know about fairies?

People have told stories and drawn pictures of fairies for hundreds of years.

The first fairies were in folk stories and they ...

- had a lot of names—the little people; the good folk; the people of peace; the fair folk. The word *fairy* is from Old French *faie*
- didn't have wings
- were small people who could do magic
- sometimes had green eyes and sometimes wore gray clothes
- were sometimes good and sometimes naughty

Today, the fairies in stories, art, theater, and movies ...

- have wings like butterflies
- have given people the idea to make fairy doors
- are usually good and help people

Could fairies be real?

Children have always asked this question. There are some famous photographs from 1918. Two children took them in their garden and they clearly show fairies! A famous writer, Sir Arthur Conan Doyle, believed the fairies were real and he wrote about them in magazines. Suddenly, the girls were famous, and the photographs were in newspapers. They were called The Cottingley Fairies.

Everyone wanted to believe that there really were fairies in the world. Much later, in 1983, the girls—then aged 65—finally said that the photos were fakes and they had used paper pictures of fairies in the photos. They were just having fun! That's a long time to keep a secret!

fake (*noun*) something that is not real
folk (*noun*) people

Phonics

Say the sounds. Read the words.

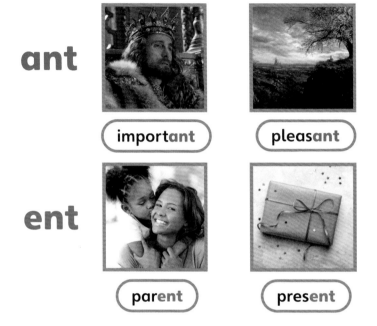

ant

important pleasant

ent

parent present

Read, then say the rhyme to a friend.

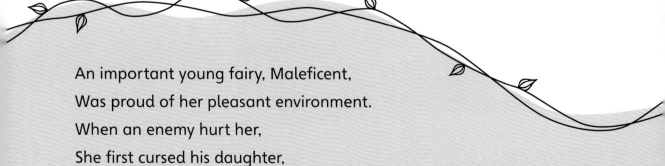

An important young fairy, Maleficent,
Was proud of her pleasant environment.
When an enemy hurt her,
She first cursed his daughter,
Then fought with her terrible parent!